LOUISE HARPER

Is It ADHD?

For Every Midlife Woman Who Feels Like She's Falling Apart

First edition

This book was professionally typeset on Reedsy.
Find out more at reedsy.com

Contents

Introduction

"Why can't I keep up?"

You've probably asked yourself that question more than once. Why do other people seem to manage life's demands with ease, while you are constantly drowning in to-do lists and missed appointments with a gnawing sense that you are falling short?

It's not because you don't care. In fact, it's quite the opposite. You care so deeply that it's exhausting. You try harder, push yourself more, stay up later, try to plan better. Yet it never feels like enough.

Maybe you've Googled ADHD at midnight, wondering if the chaos in your head is something more than just poor time management. Maybe you came across a TikTok, an Instagram reel, or a podcast where another woman described your inner world with such eerie accuracy that it made you stop and stare at your phone, heart pounding. Or perhaps you're just so tired in a way that sleep never fixes. Physically, mentally, emotionally. No matter how many early nights you try, no matter how many supplements, planners, green smoothies or well-intentioned productivity hacks you throw at it, you still feel like you are barely holding it together.

Welcome to what many are now calling a quiet epidemic. A growing number of women, particularly in their thirties, forties, and fifties, are beginning to ask themselves questions that were rarely asked a decade ago. Could this be ADHD? Is something *wrong* with me, or is this simply what it feels like to be a woman heading towards mid-life?

The truth is that many of us have spent years living in survival mode without even realising it. We have been taught, both directly and indirectly, to cope no matter what. To be capable, competent, and composed. From childhood, we were trained to meet expectations, to get it right, to behave, to perform. Some of us excelled at school. Some of us held things together at home. Many of us played the role of the "good girl" while quietly struggling behind the scenes.

We learned early to suppress the chaos and mask the cracks. We told ourselves that the problem was us. That we just needed to try harder. Get organised. Stop being so dramatic. Work on our mindset. All while managing careers, homes, children, relationships, and a constant mental to- do list that never seemed to end. And when it became too much to handle, we were told it was probably stress. Or hormones. Or that we just needed to take a bubble bath and get more sleep.

But now something is shifting, and it's social media that has helped turn the tide. The internet has become a place where women are sharing their raw truths. Late diagnoses. Emotional burnout. Hidden struggles. Stories that sound a lot like your own, almost like someone opened your brain and made a reel about it. With every post, podcast, and shared story, more women are waking up to the same realisation: this is not just me. This is bigger than me.

This book is not here to tell you who you are. It will not diagnose you. I'm not a clinician, and this is not a textbook. What it is, however, is a space for reflection, clarity, and kindness. A compassionate guide for the woman who is tired of feeling lazy, unreliable, or broken. For the woman who has spent years wondering why it all feels so much harder than it should. For the woman who suspects there is more to her story than bad habits or personal failings.

You do not need a label in order to start taking care of yourself. You do not need permission from a professional to begin making changes that work for your life and your brain. You only need the courage to stop pushing yourself to meet expectations that were never made with you in mind.

This is your permission to pause and begin treating yourself with the same compassion you offer others. You are not alone in this, and you are not failing.

You are navigating a life that was never designed for the way your mind works, and you are doing it without the support, recognition, or rest you needed.

Let's change that. Starting now.

1

Chapter 1: Why So Many Women Are Asking: "Do I Have ADHD?"

If you've ever found yourself deep down a rabbit hole of ADHD content, nodding in recognition as someone describes the scattered, overwhelming, often contradictory mess that lives in your head, you are far from alone. In recent years, something has shifted. More and more women are quietly asking themselves a question that used to seem irrelevant or even absurd:

Could I have ADHD? Could this be me?

This surge in curiosity is not a passing trend or an online fad. It is part of a wider awakening, a cultural recalibration that's long overdue. For decades, ADHD was almost exclusively understood through a narrow and stereotypical lens. It was seen as a childhood disorder, usually identified in boys who were loud, hyperactive, impulsive, and disruptive in class. These children couldn't sit still, blurted out answers, and were easy to spot. They matched the textbook symptoms. They triggered concerns and got flagged early.

Girls, on the other hand, often didn't. A girl who stared out the window, quietly daydreaming, or one who bit her nails and avoided eye contact wasn't seen as disordered. A perfectionist who rewrote her homework three times to make it "just right" or stayed up late organising her school bag for the next day didn't seem like someone struggling with a neurodevelopmental condition. She seemed like a conscientious student, maybe a little anxious or overly sensitive, but not someone who needed help. As long as she was achieving and behaving, no alarms were raised.

This is how so many women with ADHD fell through the cracks. They masked. They compensated. They worked twice as hard to keep up. They internalised their struggles and told themselves they just needed to try harder. And as adulthood set in, that internal pressure only grew. Eventually, the carefully maintained system of coping started to break down.

So why now? Why are so many women beginning to recognise these patterns for the first time in their 30s, 40s, or 50s?

One reason is life stage. This is the point where the demands often become *relentless*. Careers become more intense. Parenting responsibilities increase. Relationships mature or fall apart. The mental load of running a household, managing finances, juggling school forms and meal planning and work emails and family WhatsApps, becomes impossible to ignore. For years, many women managed to get by on sheer willpower, overcompensation, and last-minute adrenaline. But eventually, that stops working and the wheels come off.

Tasks that once felt manageable now feel overwhelming. Things slip through the cracks. Deadlines are missed. Tempers are shorter. Emotions run high. And the shame kicks in. When the usual strategies no longer work, women begin searching for answers. They start to question why everything feels so much harder than it seems to be for other people. That search often leads them to ADHD. Not because they are looking for an excuse, but because they are desperate for an explanation.

Another reason is that our understanding of ADHD is evolving. Slowly but significantly, the narrative is shifting. The focus is expanding beyond the loud and disruptive behaviours of childhood to include the more subtle, internalised symptoms that many women live with for decades without realising what they are. Inattentiveness, for example, is being understood not as simply daydreaming, but as struggling to stay focused on conversations, forgetting what you were saying mid; sentence, or finding it almost impossible to follow multi; step instructions. Emotional dysregulation is now recognised as a core feature of ADHD, not a separate issue. Rejection sensitivity, time blindness, mental fatigue, and executive dysfunction are finally being acknowledged as part of the ADHD picture. These are the things that don't always get noticed in a classroom or flagged by teachers. But they wreak havoc in adult life.

The emergence of relatable, human-centred ADHD content, especially on social media, has played a huge role. For many women, hearing someone speak candidly about forgetting to eat, struggling to reply to texts, crying over a minor setback, or feeling completely paralysed by a simple task is like recognising yourself reflected in someone else's experience. That sense of resonance, that moment of *"Oh my god, that's me"* can be the beginning of everything. It can crack open years of confusion, shame, and silence.

So yes, more women are asking the question. And for good reason. Because the version of ADHD most of us were taught to look for never included us. So many of us have spent years struggling quietly, thinking we were just flawed or chaotic or not trying hard enough. And the truth is finally surfacing in the stories we are telling each other.

And whether or not the answer to the question is ADHD, the act of asking it is powerful. It is a reclaiming. A refusal to keep pretending that your struggles don't exist just because they don't fit someone else's checklist.

The Invisibility of "High-Functioning" Women

Here's the cruel irony: many women with ADHD have flown under the radar precisely because they've been so good at hiding it. High achievers, perfectionists, people-pleasers; the kind of women who look like they've got it all together on the outside, but feel like they're barely holding on inside.

They're the ones who double-book themselves despite having a complicated calendar system. Who forget to reply to the email until 11pm, then stay up till 2am fixing it. Who burn out repeatedly but still push through. Their ADHD is hidden under layers of overcompensation; until it isn't. Eventually, the constant effort of keeping it together takes its toll, and what looked like "functioning" turns out to have been survival all along.

When they crash, they do it quietly. They burn out in silence, then blame themselves for not coping better. They tell themselves to get more sleep, try another productivity method, or be more disciplined. They rarely let anyone see the truth of their struggle. Most people around them have no idea. In fact, these women are often praised for how capable and organised they appear. But what is seen as competence is often a frantic and fragile structure held together by sheer willpower, fuelled by fear of being exposed.

This kind of "functioning" is not truly functioning at all. It is survival, dressed up as success. It is the ability to meet expectations while sacrificing rest, joy, clarity, and self; worth. It is saying yes when you want to say no. It is doing things at the last minute not because you are lazy, but because your brain genuinely struggles to initiate action without extreme urgency. It is performing well in the external world while quietly battling a constant inner voice that tells you you are falling short.

Eventually, something gives. The mask slips. The systems stop working. The exhaustion becomes unmanageable. And in that moment, what looked like high; functioning reveals itself to be something very different. It was never ease. It was effort. It was never balance. It was burnout waiting to happen.

Many women with ADHD are only recognised when that point

of collapse is reached. Not because they have become less capable, but because they can no longer maintain the illusion of coping. The diagnosis often comes not during their peak achievements, but in the fallout. When the strategies that once kept them afloat can no longer be sustained.

The tragedy is that their struggle was there all along. It just didn't look the way people expected it to. And now, they are finally being seen.

The Weight of Expectation

This is where gender really comes into play. Women are raised, consciously or not, to *cope*. To internalise rather than externalise. To work harder, be better, try again. We are taught to organise everyone else's lives, but often left unsupported in managing our own.

ADHD in women is often misread as anxiety, depression, or character flaws. Forgetfulness? You're flaky. Emotional? Too sensitive. Messy house? You're lazy. Overwhelmed? You just need to be more organised.

The problem is that this internal experience is rarely recognised for what it is. Instead of being seen as a sign of neurodivergence, it is misinterpreted. Forgetfulness is dismissed as flakiness. Emotional sensitivity is labelled as being too dramatic or irrational. A messy home or disorganised schedule is taken as laziness. Chronic overwhelm is brushed off as poor time management. These assumptions hurt. Not only are they wrong, but they place the burden of blame entirely on the individual. What is actually a neurological difference is mistaken for a lack of willpower or personal failing.

This mislabelling is deeply damaging. Because when society consistently tells you that your struggles are a reflection of your character, you start to believe it. You begin to see yourself as someone who is failing at things that others manage with ease. You push harder, trying to keep up. You hide your struggles because admitting them feels like weakness. And you live with a quiet, constant fear that one day, everyone else will realise just how much you are faking it.

Many women spend years; sometimes decades; trapped in this cycle. They become hyper-independent, hyper-responsible, and quietly exhausted. They are the ones holding everything together, but never feeling held themselves. Until, at some point, something shifts. It might be burnout. It might be an article or a conversation with a friend. It might be a podcast or a social media post that captures their exact experience in words they never had for themselves. And suddenly, something clicks. The fog lifts, even just slightly. They begin to ask questions they were never encouraged to ask before.

Could it be ADHD? Could all of this be something more than just stress or failure or being bad at life? And with that one question, a door opens. The weight of expectation begins to loosen its grip. Not all at once, and not always easily; but enough to begin. Enough to start seeing that perhaps the problem was never who they were, but what they were taught to carry in silence.

TikTok, Podcasts, and the Power of Relatability

In recent years, platforms like TikTok and Instagram have exploded with bite; sized, brutally honest ADHD content. Women are talking openly about their missed diagnoses, their childhood masking, their chaotic adult lives. They're showing what ADHD looks like *in real time*, in the home, in motherhood, in careers; and it's radically different from the outdated textbook examples.

And it resonates. Women are seeing themselves reflected for the first time. Not as broken, but as misunderstood.

So, if you're asking yourself, "Do I have ADHD?" you're not imagining things, and you're not jumping on a trend. You're part of a wider awakening. You're tuning into something that's been waiting for attention for a long time.

And whether or not you ever get a diagnosis, that self-inquiry matters. Because recognising that your struggles are real, and not a personal failing, is the first step in giving yourself the support you've long deserved.

2

Chapter 2: The Triple Trap – ADHD, Hormones & Burnout

You're overstimulated and underpowered at the same time. You try to rest, but the tiredness never seems to shift. You lie down, but your mind stays on full volume. You're worn out, yet somehow still wired.

This is what I call the Triple Trap. It's the tangled web of ADHD (whether diagnosed or not), hormonal shifts, and chronic burnout all overlapping in a way that makes it nearly impossible to tell where one ends and the next begins. Each one fuels the others. Each one drains you in different ways.

You might be navigating a workday with brain fog, emotional sensitivity, and a nervous system stuck on high alert. You might be crying in the car after school drop-off and then walking into work with a smile like nothing happened. You might be trying to remember what you walked into a room for, while your heart is racing and your patience is at breaking point; and you're still telling yourself you just need to get more organised.

And the thing is, this triple layer of struggle is rarely acknowledged properly. ADHD in women is still under diagnosed. Hormonal changes, especially during perimenopause, are brushed off as moodiness or ageing. Burnout is normalised, especially for women who are holding households, families, careers, and mental loads without a break. Put all of that together, and of course you feel like you're falling apart. Of course you're forgetful. Of course you're struggling to focus, to sleep, to make decisions, or feel like yourself.

But because you're still showing up and getting things done; maybe not as gracefully as you used to, but still functioning enough that no one sees how heavy it all is. You might not even fully see it yourself, because you've been carrying it for so long, it just feels normal. Until it doesn't.

The Triple Trap creates a kind of static in the system. ADHD throws off your focus, emotional regulation, and ability to manage time. Hormones disrupt everything from your energy levels to your sleep to your cognitive sharpness. And burnout chips away at your motivation, joy, and ability to bounce back from stress. It's a loop that keeps feeding itself. You try harder, you fall further behind, you burn out more deeply, and still you feel like it's your fault.

You are not disorganised. You are not weak. You are not overreacting. You are managing a neurological load, a biological shift, and an emotional exhaustion all at once. And you're probably doing it with very little validation or support. If you feel like your brain has been in overdrive for years and your body just can't keep up, you're not imagining it. This tangled knot of symptoms is real. And the first step in untangling it is simply recognising what you're dealing with.

You don't have to sort it all out overnight. You don't need to have all the answers. But naming the Triple Trap for what it is can bring huge relief. You are not broken. You are operating under conditions that would challenge anyone. And the more you understand that, the more space you create to start doing things differently and on your own terms.

ADHD's Many Companions

ADHD doesn't tend to show up on its own. For a lot of women, it brings a few extra "friends" along for the ride; anxiety, low energy, chronic fatigue, trouble sleeping, and that constant, uncomfortable feeling of being behind, even when you're doing your best. You might not even realise you're dealing with more than one thing, because the symptoms blend together so easily. It becomes your normal. A hard, overwhelming kind of normal.

It's the quiet panic that follows you through the day. That hum of *"What have I forgotten now?"* or *"Why can't I just get it together?"* You might not be visibly falling apart, but inside, you feel like you're constantly spinning plates. And even when you do manage to keep them all going, it doesn't feel like enough.

This kind of mental pressure builds up. It's draining. You might go through your whole day juggling meetings, appointments, and responsibilities, only to get to the end of it completely wiped out. But then, when it's time to rest, your brain kicks back into gear. You're lying in bed at 2am, replaying that one weird thing you said in a meeting or worrying about something on your to-do list that you forgot to write down. You're shattered, but somehow still buzzing. Tired and wired, all at once.

This is the cycle so many women are stuck in. You push through because you have to. You put on a face, keep it together, show up for everyone else; and then you crash, only to wake up and do it all again. It's no wonder so many women end up feeling anxious, exhausted, and confused about why they can't seem to "get on top of things," no matter how hard they try.

The emotional weight of all this is heavy. And the longer it goes on, the more you start to wonder what's wrong with you. Why is everyone else coping when you're falling apart over the laundry? Why does your brain feel like it's in a constant state of chaos, even when life looks manageable on paper?

And then there's the guilt. Guilt for being tired. Guilt for not remembering. Guilt for snapping at someone when you didn't mean to. Guilt for needing rest but not being able to relax. It piles on, and most of the time, you just blame yourself. You think you're just not trying hard enough, or you're not naturally organised, or that you're somehow not built for "normal" life. But that's not it.

What you're feeling is what happens when ADHD goes unrecognised and unsupported for years. It's what happens when your brain is constantly working overtime just to keep up. And that feeling of being anxious, tired, overwhelmed, and like you're always dropping the ball? That's not laziness. That's your nervous system telling you it's had enough.

You're not weak. You're not a mess. You're not failing. You're running a marathon in your head every single day while still doing all the things people expect of you. And no one else can see it, because you've gotten so good at hiding the effort it takes.

So if you're asking yourself *"Why am I like this?"* - this might be part of the answer. And no, you're not imagining it. It's real. It's valid. And most importantly, you're not the only one.

For many women, this all ramps up in their late 30s and 40s - and that's no coincidence. Because this is also when hormonal shifts begin to stir.

The Perimenopause Puzzle: When Hormones Hijack the Brain

Here comes the second layer of the trap, and it's one that catches many women completely off guard: fluctuating hormones.

Perimenopause is the stretch of time leading up to menopause, and while it's more commonly associated with women in their forties, it can begin much earlier. For some, subtle changes can start in their mid-thirties, though they often go unnoticed or are brushed off as unrelated stress. This phase can last for years, and it brings with it a slow, frustrating unravelling of the way your mind and body used to work.

Oestrogen and progesterone, two key hormones that decline and fluctuate during perimenopause, aren't just about fertility or reproduction. These hormones are deeply connected to brain function. Oestrogen, in particular, plays a major role in regulating dopamine, the neurotransmitter that helps with motivation, focus, and emotional regulation. All of these are areas already impacted by ADHD, so when oestrogen levels drop or swing unpredictably, things can get a whole lot worse.

You might suddenly find yourself dealing with brain fog that makes even simple tasks feel mentally slippery. Words escape you in conversation. You walk into rooms and forget why. Your short-term memory starts to feel like a sieve. Organisation, which might have always been a challenge, now feels impossible. You may also notice you're more emotionally reactive. Small things can bring tears or frustration that feel out of proportion, and your ability to bounce back after a stressful moment feels slower. Focus might become patchy, and your motivation may disappear entirely some days. And then there's sleep; the thing you used to rely on to reset. Now, it's light, restless, or interrupted by 3am wakeups that leave you staring at the ceiling for hours.

What's most frustrating is how easy it is for these changes to be dismissed. You're told it's just stress, or you're getting older, or you need to try meditation or take a vitamin. But if you already have ADHD, or have been unknowingly managing the symptoms without a name, this stage of life can feel like hitting a wall. Things you were once able to push through with effort or adrenaline might now feel completely overwhelming. The cracks get harder to patch over. What used to feel like background noise becomes a blaring alarm.

This isn't imagined. You're not making it up. And you're not the only one. For many women, perimenopause is the moment when ADHD symptoms become loud enough to notice. It's not that they weren't there before. It's just that your brain and body no longer have the hormonal buffer that helped keep things (barely) in check.

Cortisol: The Burnout Hormone

Now let's talk about the third layer of this exhausting puzzle: burnout. And this isn't the kind of burnout that goes away with a weekend off or a good night's sleep. This is long; term, chronic burnout that builds slowly over time and eventually consumes everything.

Cortisol is your body's main stress hormone. It's not all bad. In short bursts, cortisol helps you get through challenges. It gets you out of bed in the morning, helps you power through deadlines, and gives you a bit of edge in stressful situations. But when your life is one long stretch of constant juggling: managing a household, working full time, caring for others, dealing with financial stress, emotional labour, and a brain that's already working against the current, cortisol never gets the chance to settle. It stays elevated. Your body forgets how to feel safe or relaxed.

When that happens, your system begins to short-circuit. You wake up feeling tired, even after a full night's sleep. You start to feel overwhelmed by simple things, like a sink full of dishes or a cluttered inbox. You find yourself crying for no clear reason or snapping at people you love over minor things. Your emotional regulation, already challenged by ADHD, becomes even shakier.

Your nervous system is stretched thin. You might crash in the afternoon, struggling to stay awake, only to find yourself wide awake and buzzing with restless energy in the middle of the night.

And because you're still getting through the day: still showing up to work, still doing the school run, still crossing things off your list, people assume you're fine. But what they can't see is that you're running on fumes, held together by willpower and caffeine and the fear of what will happen if you stop. You've adapted so well to this state of stress that it's become your default, even though it's slowly wearing you down.

This kind of burnout doesn't shout. It whispers. It hides behind productivity and smiles, and that phrase you've probably used too many times: "I'm just tired." But it is real. And it is not sustainable.

When ADHD, fluctuating hormones, and burnout collide, it can feel like your brain and body are in open rebellion. And if you've been feeling like you're unravelling or losing your grip, it isn't just in your head. It's happening in your nervous system, in your neurotransmitters, in your lived reality. The only thing you've done wrong is believing you should be able to carry it all without support.

When All Roads Lead to Exhaustion but Nobody Sees It

This is the trap so many women find themselves in. ADHD makes life harder to manage. Hormones destabilise the brain further. Burnout strips away the last reserves of energy. And through it all, you're expected to carry on. Smile. Function. Be productive. Be pleasant. Keep going.

The result? Deep, soul-level exhaustion. A sense of being lost, unmoored, and unable to keep pace. You might question your memory, your abilities, even your sanity. But the problem isn't *you*; it's the relentless pressure to perform while your brain and body are quietly screaming for support.

This chapter isn't here to give you a diagnosis or a checklist. It's here to give you *context*. If you've been feeling like you're constantly "off," like you're trying to run a marathon in quicksand, there's likely more going on than meets the eye.

The good news? There's a way through it. But it starts by recognising that you're not imagining things. You're not just hormonal. You're not failing at life. You're navigating a perfect storm; and now that you can see it clearly, you can start to find your way out.

When All Roads Lead to Exhaustion but Nobody Sees It

This is the trap that catches so many women, and often the ones who seem like they're managing just fine. ADHD makes the day to day harder to navigate. Hormones start to shift, creating even more instability in your brain and body. And burnout chips away at what little energy and focus you have left. Together, they create a kind of silent storm that rages just beneath the surface of your life. And still, you're expected to show up. To be calm, capable, efficient, friendly, reliable, organised, and emotionally available.

So you smile when you don't feel like smiling. You keep functioning when you're falling apart inside. You stay productive when your brain is screaming for rest. You keep going because people are counting on you. You might even think that if you just try harder, things will settle down. But they don't. Instead, you reach a level of tired that isn't just physical. It's deep; the kind of exhaustion that doesn't go away after a weekend off or a few early nights.

You might start to question everything. Your memory, your intelligence, your ability to cope. You feel scattered and forgetful. You can't finish tasks, or you lose track of things mid-sentence. You wonder why you can't keep up the way you used to. It feels like everyone else is moving forward while you're stuck treading water. At times, you may even question your sanity, wondering if it really is all in your head.

But the truth is, the problem is not you. It's the pressure. The constant expectation that you will continue to perform at full capacity while your brain and body are trying to send out an SOS. It's being told to just "get more sleep" or "take a break" when what you really need is a complete reset, a new way of living that supports your wiring instead of ignoring it.

What you are experiencing is not a weakness. It's a response to years of pushing through, of masking your struggles, of surviving instead of thriving. You've been living under strain for so long that the weight of it has started to blur into the background. It's become part of your everyday. But it's not sustainable, and it doesn't have to be this way.

This chapter isn't here to hand you a diagnosis. It's not here to give you a neat checklist or a final answer. What it offers instead is context. Because once you understand what's happening beneath the surface, things start to make sense. You begin to realise that you're not lazy or weak or doing life wrong. You're reacting to a perfect storm that no one taught you how to navigate.

The good news is that there is a way through it. It starts with recognising that what you're feeling is valid. That it's not hormones or stress or being disorganised, but years of operating in survival mode, often without anyone noticing, and without enough support.

You don't need to keep pretending that everything is fine. You don't need to keep carrying this alone. Once you can see the storm clearly, you can start to chart a path out of it. One step at a time. One breath at a time. Starting now.

3

Chapter 3: Growing Up Undiagnosed

If you grew up with undiagnosed ADHD, chances are, nobody even suspected a thing. You might have been labelled "daydreamy," "emotional," or "a bit disorganised." But you weren't the child climbing the furniture or throwing tantrums in class; so you flew under the radar.

For many girls, ADHD doesn't show up the way people expect. It's not always about being hyperactive or disruptive. In fact, it often presents as the opposite: quiet, well-behaved, and overly anxious to please.

When ADHD Doesn't Look Like ADHD

That classic image of ADHD: the fidgety boy bouncing in his chair, blurting out answers, constantly interrupting, is the one that shaped how most people, including doctors and teachers, came to understand the condition. But that image was never designed with girls in mind. It's not that girls didn't have ADHD. It's just that their symptoms didn't fit the mould, so they were often missed, misunderstood, or simply ignored.

For many girls, ADHD doesn't show up in loud or disruptive ways. It hides. It adapts. It blends into the background as something else entirely. What looks like daydreaming might actually be inattentiveness. That inability to focus on dull or repetitive tasks gets written off as a lack of discipline or laziness. Racing thoughts, emotional intensity, and constant anxiety often get brushed aside as being overly sensitive, hormonal, or dramatic.

Here's what it often looked like instead:

- Getting lost in thought during lessons or conversations and being labelled as distracted or spacey
- Scrambling to finish homework or assignments at the very last minute, not because you didn't care, but because your brain simply couldn't get started until the pressure was high enough
- Being overly emotional, crying easily, or taking criticism to heart, which others chalked up to moodiness or immaturity
- Struggling with an inner restlessness; your mind is constantly buzzing, but your body is sitting still
- Talking too much in some situations to overcompensate, and zoning out completely in others
- Losing things, forgetting tasks, missing steps in instructions, and constantly being told to "pay attention"

None of these things raised alarms. They didn't disrupt the classroom. They didn't draw the kind of attention that leads to an ADHD diagnosis. Instead, they were explained away as quirks, as personality traits, or as evidence that you just weren't trying hard enough. Teachers might have told you that you were smart, but not working to your potential. Parents might have said you were careless or too sensitive. And because nobody thought to look any deeper, you internalised the idea that something was wrong with you.

The truth is, the signs were there all along. They were just easy to miss. Easy to dismiss. Especially in girls who were quiet, well; behaved, and eager to please. If you weren't acting out or causing problems, your struggles stayed hidden. You were rewarded for masking and pushing through.

So if you're only now recognising yourself in descriptions of ADHD, that's because the system wasn't built to see you. And now that you can see it for yourself, you're finally in a position to understand what's *really* been going on beneath the surface all this time.

People Pleasing, Perfectionism, and Fear of Failure

When no one recognises what's going on, and there's no support or understanding in place, many girls end up developing coping strategies that look a lot like simply being "good." Maybe you became the one who never caused trouble. The one who followed the rules, tried hard, smiled politely, and did her best to meet every expectation placed on her.

You probably learned early on to become hyper-aware of how others saw you. You might have made it your mission to be liked, to be helpful, to be impressive. You worked hard to seem fine, even when you weren't. And in doing so, you started building an identity around keeping it all together.

This might have shown up in all sorts of ways:

- Working twice as hard as your peers just to stay on track, especially when your focus kept slipping
- Over-preparing for simple tasks or procrastinating for so long that you ended up in a panic
- Treating every small mistake like a personal failure and beating yourself up over things no one else even noticed
- Relying on achievement, praise, or approval to feel good about yourself
- Avoiding risks or new challenges altogether because the idea of getting something wrong felt unbearable

What's difficult is that many of these behaviours are rewarded. People praise you for being conscientious, high-achieving, reliable, or easy to get along with. But underneath all that praise is a cost most people don't see. You start to associate being accepted with staying quiet about your struggles. You learn that love and approval are things you have to earn by keeping everything in check.

And of course, you can't keep it all in check forever. At some point, you miss a deadline. You forget something important. You have a meltdown. And when that happens, you turn on yourself. You blame your lack of discipline, your emotions, your inability to cope.

Because no one ever told you your brain might just work differently.

The Toll of Masking

All of this is part of something called masking. It's the act of covering up or hiding your symptoms so that you can blend in, avoid judgment, and meet the expectations of others. Masking isn't always something you do consciously. Sometimes it becomes so deeply ingrained that you don't even realise you're doing it. But that doesn't make it any less exhausting.

Masking can show up in a lot of different ways:

- Copying the behaviour of others to fit in socially, even if it feels unnatural
- Pushing yourself to follow routines that don't actually work for your brain
- Holding in emotional reactions so you can appear calm, logical, or "put together"
- Pretending everything is fine when inside you're overwhelmed, confused, or on the verge of shutting down

Doing this day after day, year after year, takes a toll. Your self; esteem begins to wear thin. You start to feel like there's something wrong with you, because everyone else seems to handle life so much more easily. You begin to wonder if you're broken. Over time, this kind of emotional suppression can lead to anxiety, depression, and a kind of lingering shame that's hard to name but always present.

One of the most painful parts of masking is how effective it can be. You become so good at looking capable that people stop looking any deeper. And because they don't see your struggle, they assume there isn't one. Which means the support you actually need never comes.

That's why so many women with ADHD only get diagnosed later in life. The signs were there. The effort was real. But the mask worked too well. And when you're constantly hiding the truth about how hard things are, even from yourself, it becomes harder to ask for help. You end up thinking you're the problem; when really, you were just doing your best to survive in a world that never understood you were struggling.

Understanding the Past Without Getting Stuck There

Looking back on your childhood through the lens of ADHD can be a confronting experience. It's common to grieve what could've been; what might have changed if someone had noticed earlier, or if you'd been given the right tools and understanding.

But while your past can explain a lot, it doesn't have to define your future.

Recognising the patterns is the first step toward healing. When you see that the "flaws" you've internalised were actually coping strategies, a different picture begins to emerge. You weren't lazy, dramatic, or disorganised. You were doing your best with an invisible difference that no one helped you understand.

And now, as an adult, you have the opportunity to rewrite the story. Not by pretending the past didn't happen; but by refusing to carry its blame any further.

You don't need to keep performing perfection. You don't need to keep masking your struggles. You're allowed to be who you are and still be worthy of support, success, and peace.

The girl you were did what she had to do to survive. The woman you are now gets to choose a different way forward.

4

Chapter 4: You're Not Lazy – You're Wired Differently

How many times have you called yourself lazy?

You look around at the dishes piled up, the unread emails, the half-finished laundry, and you wonder why, *despite your best intentions,* you still haven't "sorted your life out." You beat yourself up for being inconsistent, for letting things slide, for not doing what you said you would. You tell yourself you're failing.

But what if it's not laziness? What if your brain just works differently?

The Myth of Laziness

"Lazy" is one of the most damaging and misleading labels you can place on yourself. It carries a heavy weight. It suggests you don't care. That you aren't trying. That you're choosing not to act. But for women dealing with ADHD, this couldn't be further from the truth.

Most of the time, the problem isn't that you don't care. It's that you care *too* much. You care about doing things properly. You care about not letting people down. You care about making things perfect. But the more you care, the more overwhelming it becomes. The pressure builds until you can't even start. And from the outside, that looks like laziness. On the inside, though, it's something else entirely.

What people often read as "not doing anything" is usually a complicated mix of things like:

- Struggling to begin a task because your brain can't find a starting point
- Feeling completely drained from the constant mental noise and effort it takes just to function
- Losing track of time and missing windows of opportunity because time feels slippery and abstract
- Avoiding tasks out of fear that you'll get it wrong, mess it up, or be criticised
- Getting stuck in a loop of shame after even small mistakes, which makes it harder to try again

You're not sitting around doing nothing because you don't want to be productive. You're not avoiding tasks because you're careless. You're stuck because your brain is overwhelmed. You're frozen because you've hit a wall you can't explain. The task in front of you might be something simple: sending an email, booking an appointment, putting laundry away, but it feels like too much. Like trying to climb a mountain without any idea where the path starts.

This isn't laziness. It's executive dysfunction and exhaustion from years of forcing yourself to function in a way that doesn't work for you.

What ADHD Feels Like in Older Women

You might struggle with emotional regulation. Something small, like a comment from your manager or a partner forgetting to text, can hit you hard and linger for hours. You might find yourself crying over something that doesn't seem like a big deal, then feeling embarrassed or confused by your reaction. You might snap quickly or withdraw without meaning to.

Your focus may be all over the place. One minute you're zoning out in a meeting or forgetting what someone just said. Next, you're obsessively organising a drawer or researching a niche hobby for hours without a break. It's not that you can't focus. It's that you can't always control *what* you focus on or *when*.

Time is slippery. You either think something will take five minutes and it takes an hour, or you lose track of hours entirely while scrolling or trying to get one small thing done. Planning your day feels like guesswork. Deadlines sneak up on you. You always feel like you're running behind, even when you're technically on time.

Then there's task paralysis. You sit there, staring at a to; do list, knowing what you need to do but feeling completely unable to begin. The longer you wait, the worse it feels. And when you *do* manage to get things done, you often swing into overdrive to catch up, saying yes to everything and taking on more than you can handle. Eventually, the crash comes, and you're back to square one.

The result is a kind of emotional whiplash. You swing between being overly responsible and completely shut down. You manage to do incredible things some days, and the next day you're frozen by the thought of answering an email. And then you judge yourself for both. You feel guilty when you're doing too little, and resentful when you're doing too much.

If this sounds familiar, you're not alone. And you're definitely not lazy. You're someone whose brain is trying to function in a world that often doesn't recognise how hard you're already working just to stay upright.

From To-Do List Shame to Self-Compassion

For many neurodivergent women, to-do lists come with more baggage than they should. You sit down, write out everything that needs doing, and feel a little spark of hope. Maybe this will be the day it all gets sorted. Maybe this time you'll stay on track. But then the day unfolds, things go off-script, and the list just stares back at you. Every unchecked box feels like a quiet accusation. You end the day feeling like you've failed again. And yet, without the list, things unravel even faster. It's a frustrating cycle that feels impossible to win.

But what if the list wasn't a measure of your worth? What if it was simply a tool, a gentle reminder instead of a test you're destined to fail? What if the point of writing things down wasn't to prove how productive you can be, but to support your brain in a way that actually helps?

Everything starts to change when you shift from judgement to curiosity. When you look at your patterns not as flaws, but as information. You might start noticing things like this:

- You are perfectly capable of getting things done, but only when there's urgency, excitement, or a sense of novelty
- You thrive when there's some external structure like a deadline, a colleague checking in, or a friend doing the task with you
- You need movement, stimulation, or some kind of dopamine boost to get going. No amount of guilt or self-criticism will flip that switch for you
- You are not unmotivated. You are not a mess. You are not broken. You're carrying an invisible load, and trying to move through a world that wasn't designed with your brain in mind

Self-compassion doesn't mean you stop caring about your responsibilities. It doesn't mean you give up. What it *does* mean is building systems that support you, rather than shame you into submission. It means asking, "What do I need to make this feel easier?" instead of "Why can't I just do it like everyone else?"

Productivity Is Not Your Worth

We live in a world that rewards output. The more you do, the more valuable you are; or at least, that's what we've been told. It's a system that praises long hours, busy schedules, and endless goals, while looking down on anything that resembles rest, softness, or struggle. And for women with ADHD, or anyone dealing with long-term burnout, that belief system is harmful. It tells you that if you are not producing, you are not enough.

That mindset turns downtime into guilt. It turns mental fatigue into a character flaw. It takes your very real neurological differences and dresses them up as laziness, inconsistency, or lack of discipline. It makes you believe that if you just worked harder, pushed more, or tried again, everything would fall into place.

But your worth isn't something you earn by completing tasks. You are not a machine. You are a human being with a unique brain, one that needs different tools and rhythms to function at its best. And just because your path doesn't look like everyone else's doesn't mean it's any less valid.

Letting go of the idea that productivity defines your value is not easy. It takes time. It takes unlearning. But it is necessary. Because you are already worthy, whether or not your inbox is empty, whether or not your kitchen is tidy, whether or not your to-do list got done today.

You don't need to prove anything to rest. You don't need to feel guilty for needing help or taking a slower route. You don't need to wrestle with your brain every day to deserve support and understanding.

You are not lazy. You are wired differently. And that's not a problem to fix. It's a reality to honour.

5

Chapter 5: Self-Diagnosis vs. Clinical Diagnosis

By the time many women start seriously questioning whether they might have ADHD, they've already done hours of research, completed countless online quizzes, and had several "holy crap, that's me" moments listening to podcasts or scrolling TikTok.

And yet, when it comes to taking that next step: seeking a formal diagnosis, things often get murky.

Do you *need* a clinical diagnosis to validate your experience?

There are no one-size-fits-all answers, but there *are* things to consider. And whether you decide to go down the formal route or not, your experience is still valid.

Should You Get Assessed?

This is often the big question, the one that lingers in the background once you've started to recognise some of your own experiences in ADHD stories:

Should I get a formal assessment?

It really depends on what you need, what you have access to, and what feels right for you personally. For some women, getting a diagnosis can be an incredibly validating and helpful step. It can offer a sense of clarity, a name for what you've been going through, and a kind of closure that helps bring your past into focus.

A clinical diagnosis can also open doors. It can give you access to medication, therapy, and support that might otherwise be out of reach. It can make workplace adjustments more straightforward. And if you've spent years feeling broken, misunderstood, or like you're constantly falling short, hearing someone say "this is real" can bring a sense of deep relief. It can help you speak about your experience with more confidence, not just to others, but to yourself.

But it's also important to be honest about what the process can look like. A diagnosis is not always a quick or easy path. It's not a magic fix, and for many women, the journey can be frustrating, expensive, and emotionally draining.

The Reality Check: Diagnosis Isn't Always Simple

This is something a lot of people don't realise until they're already in the thick of it. Getting assessed for ADHD as an adult woman often isn't straightforward. In fact, it can feel like another uphill battle.

If you're in the UK and going through the NHS, the wait times are long. Really long. Some women are waiting two to four years just for their initial assessment. That's not an exaggeration; it's the current reality for many.

Private assessments are available and typically much faster, but they come with a high price tag. You're often looking at somewhere between £600 and £1,200, sometimes more, depending on the clinic and the type of report they provide.

If you're in the UK and going through the NHS, the wait times for an adult ADHD assessment can be extremely long. This isn't a slight delay; it's often a matter of years. Some women are being told they'll need to wait two to four years just for an initial appointment. In some areas, people are being referred to waiting lists that are already closed to new patients because the demand has outpaced capacity so dramatically. This delay is frustrating at best and deeply distressing at worst, especially if you're already in crisis or at breaking point.

There is an option in England to request assessment under the NHS Right to Choose scheme, which allows you to be referred to an external provider like Psychiatry UK or ADHD360 by your GP. This route is often quicker than local NHS services, though it still involves a wait it's often several months rather than several years. However, it only applies if you are registered with a GP in England, and not all GPs are familiar with how the Right to Choose process works, so some persistence may be needed.

Private assessments in the UK are usually much faster. You can often be seen within a few weeks. But this speed comes at a cost. The typical price for a full diagnostic assessment ranges from around £600 to £1,200, depending on the provider, the region, and whether they include post-diagnosis support or follow-up appointments. Some clinics offer a lower-cost option for a single appointment and written report, while others include more comprehensive support packages. It's important to research carefully and ensure the provider is qualified and follows national diagnostic guidelines (such as those from NICE).

In Ireland, public access to adult ADHD diagnosis is very limited and often inconsistent, depending on the county and the availability of services. Most adults seeking a diagnosis end up going private. Costs tend to be broadly similar to the UK, with assessments typically priced between €600 and €1,200. However, waitlists for private clinics can still be several months long, due to rising demand and limited specialist availability.

In Australia, ADHD assessment for adults is becoming more common, but the system is still under strain. Medicare does not routinely cover ADHD diagnosis and treatment for adults, which means many people need to go private. Costs vary depending on the state and clinic, but assessments typically range from AUD $800 to $2,000. Accessing medication after diagnosis can also be a challenge, as prescribing rules differ by state and many GPs are hesitant or restricted from prescribing ADHD medication without a specialist's input. Public waiting lists exist but are often years long, and access can depend on whether services for adult ADHD are available in your region at all.

In New Zealand, adult ADHD services through the public health system are patchy. Some district health boards do offer assessments, but the process can be slow and inconsistent. Wait times vary depending on the region and local resources, and not all public mental health services provide adult ADHD assessments at all. As a result, many people go private, with costs typically ranging from NZD $800 to $1,500. Medication access also tends to require ongoing review by a psychiatrist, at least initially.

In Canada, ADHD is considered a medical condition and therefore covered by public healthcare, but the experience depends heavily on the province and whether you can access the right professionals. In provinces with fewer psychiatrists or longer wait times, you may still wait one to two years for an assessment through the public system. In Ontario, for example, assessments are covered by OHIP, but many adults end up on lengthy waiting lists. In provinces like British Columbia or Alberta, there is growing reliance on private clinics, where assessments range from CAD $1,000 to $2,500 depending on the provider and what's included.

In the United States, ADHD assessment is almost always

done through private healthcare, unless you are covered by Medicaid or a specific insurance plan that includes mental health assessments. Costs in the US are highly variable but often high - ranging from USD $700 to $2,500 or more. Insurance may cover part of the assessment, but many plans require significant out of pocket costs or do not include ADHD-specific testing at all. That said, access is generally faster than in public systems elsewhere, if you can afford to pay or are well insured. Some people choose to go through psychologists or psychiatrists, while others access diagnosis through ADHD; specialised clinics or even telehealth services.

The overall trend is clear: demand for adult ADHD diagnosis is growing, especially among women, but the healthcare systems have not yet caught up. This is leading many to seek private assessments out of necessity, not luxury. And while some people do find clarity and relief through the private route, others are simply priced out or left waiting for years in systems that were never designed to support them. It's not fair. It's not your fault. And unfortunately, it's a very common experience.

If you're considering assessment, it can help to connect with local ADHD communities online or through support groups. They often have up; to; date information on wait times, costs, and trusted providers in your region. Whether you decide to pursue diagnosis now or not, just knowing that you're not alone in this process can be a lifeline.

And even once you're in the room with a professional, there's still no guarantee of being heard. Medical gaslighting is, unfortunately, a common experience for many women. If you're articulate, high-functioning, or have managed to hold things together on the surface, your concerns might be brushed off or redirected. You might be told it's just anxiety, or depression, or that you're simply overwhelmed from trying to do too much. And yes, you might *be* anxious or overwhelmed, but that doesn't mean ADHD isn't there too.

Another issue is the criteria used for diagnosis. Most of it is still built around how ADHD presents in young boys. So if your symptoms don't match that template, you may feel unseen, even when everything you're describing is valid.

None of this is meant to put you off seeking a diagnosis if that's what you want to do. For many women, it's absolutely worth it. But it's important to go into the process with your eyes open. Some women come out of their assessment feeling empowered and finally understood. Others walk away feeling dismissed, confused, or even more uncertain than before.

If you do decide to seek a diagnosis, it's helpful to prepare. Keep notes, track your symptoms, bring specific examples, and, if possible, bring someone who knows you well and can help you advocate for yourself. And remember, whatever the outcome, your experience is real. The challenges you face are real. A diagnosis can help explain them; but it doesn't define your worth, and it isn't the only way to start making your life work better for you.

What You Can Do in the Meantime

If you're not ready or able to pursue a formal ADHD assessment right now, that doesn't mean you have to stay stuck. You don't need a diagnosis to begin understanding your brain or finding ways to make life feel a little more manageable. There are practical, supportive steps you can take right now, even without the paperwork or professional validation.

Online Screeners

One helpful starting point is using self-assessment tools. The ASRS (Adult ADHD Self-Report Scale), which is often used in clinical settings, and the ADHD 2.0 screener can give you a clearer picture of how ADHD traits may be showing up in your life. These tools are not meant to diagnose you, but they *are* used by many professionals as part of the diagnostic process. They can help you put language to experiences you've long struggled to explain, and they often offer that first glimmer of, *"Oh... this isn't just me."*

Peer Support

There's something uniquely powerful about connecting with others who just *get it*. Online ADHD communities, forums, and support groups can be an enormous source of relief and validation. Hearing other women describe the exact things you've been silently battling can take a huge weight off your shoulders. Whether it's a Facebook group, Reddit thread, Discord community, or local meetup, finding people who speak your language and live your experience is healing in a way that can't always be measured. These spaces are where many women begin to feel truly seen for the first time.

Coaching and Therapy

You don't need a diagnosis to benefit from ADHD coaching or therapeutic support. Many ADHD coaches specialise in working with people who are exploring their traits or managing symptoms without a formal label. They can offer tools for managing overwhelm, building structure, improving focus, and finding your own rhythms. Some therapists also understand ADHD well and can help with related challenges like emotional regulation, anxiety, low self-esteem, or the impact of years of masking.

Look for professionals who are neurodiversity-affirming and who recognise that ADHD doesn't always look like the textbook definition. Whether your support comes through coaching, counselling, or a combination of both, it's entirely valid to seek help without having a diagnosis on file.

Self-Education

Sometimes the most empowering thing you can do is simply start learning. There are brilliant books, podcasts, articles, and videos that break down ADHD in clear, relatable ways. You can learn about how executive dysfunction works, why you might struggle with motivation or emotional regulation, how dopamine plays a role in your energy and focus, and how to gently shift your routines to suit your actual brain, not the one the world expects you to have.

Educating yourself helps to reduce the shame. It creates space for self-understanding instead of self-blame. And even if no one else validates your experience yet, that knowledge becomes an anchor. It gives you the language and insight to start making informed choices about how you work, how you rest, and how you take care of yourself.

You don't have to wait for someone in a white coat to tell you what you already feel in your bones. You can begin making changes now.

Diagnosis Is a Tool, Not a Requirement

Getting a formal diagnosis can absolutely be valuable. For some women, it's a huge turning point; a moment of clarity that helps them rewrite the stories they've been told about themselves for years. But it's important to remember that a diagnosis is just one tool. It is not the only path to understanding, healing, or change.

What matters most is learning how *your* brain works. What it needs to feel safe, focused, and calm. What helps you function, and what sends you into shutdown. You don't need a professional to give you permission to do that. You are allowed to know yourself. You are allowed to support yourself. You are allowed to start building a life that suits your needs, with or without a diagnosis.

For many women, self-diagnosis is not about jumping on a trend or trying to find an excuse. It's about finally naming something that has been there for years and giving yourself *permission*. Permission to stop pushing through. Permission to stop pretending everything is fine. Permission to stop believing that you're failing just because you function differently.

Whether you have a formal diagnosis, are still exploring the possibility, or are just beginning to question what's been going on beneath the surface, your experience is valid. Your struggle is real. And you deserve support, whatever path you choose.

So, should you seek a diagnosis? Maybe. Maybe not.

But don't let the system's slowness, cost, or dismissiveness become another reason to abandon yourself. Whether you pursue a formal path or not, your story matters. Your brain matters. Your *experience* matters.

And you don't need a doctor to tell you that something's been off; you've lived it. That alone is enough to begin the work of supporting yourself with compassion, clarity, and care.

6

Chapter 6: ADHD-Friendly Tools That Actually Help

If you've ever bought a planner with the hope that *this* one would change your life, only to abandon it within a week, you're not alone.

So many productivity tools are designed for neurotypical brains: structured, linear, reward-driven by long-term outcomes. But ADHD doesn't work like that. And if you keep trying to use systems that work *against* your brain instead of *with* it, you'll just keep reinforcing the same message: "I can't stick to anything."

That's not true. The problem isn't you. The problem is the system.

This chapter is about tools that actually *work* because they're rooted in how the ADHD brain functions, not in how it's expected to behave.

Designing Guilt-Free Systems

The first rule of ADHD-friendly systems? They have to be *flexible*. Rigid routines and high-pressure accountability often backfire. You need something adaptable. Something that forgives off days and rewards momentum, not perfection.

Ask yourself:

- What *actually helps* me start a task when I'm frozen?
- What environment helps me *focus*, not just sit there scrolling?
- What *has worked before*, even temporarily, and why?

Your systems shouldn't make you feel guilty. They should feel like scaffolding, not shackles. The goal is to *support* your energy and motivation, not make you feel worse.

Time Blindness, Forgetfulness & Emotional Overwhelm

These are three core ADHD experiences that wreak havoc on daily life:

Time blindness means you struggle to sense the passage of time. Ten minutes can feel like an hour, or vice versa. This leads to chronic lateness, last-minute panics, and scheduling disasters.

Forgetfulness isn't about being careless. ADHD brains struggle with working memory. You might forget why you opened the fridge, miss appointments, or lose track of mid; task steps.

Emotional overwhelm can hit hard. Whether it's rejection sensitivity, sensory overload, or the shame spiral of feeling behind, emotional regulation becomes a daily battle.

But you're not doomed to chaos. These issues can be managed with tools tailored to your needs; and without expecting yourself to become a colour-coded superwoman overnight.

Simple Tools That Actually Make a Difference

Body Doubling

This is a game-changer. Simply being in the presence of someone else, virtually or in person, can make it easier to start tasks. There's something about having another person "holding the space" that quiets the panic and helps you get on with it. Try virtual co-working sessions, silent Zoom rooms, or even texting a friend to say, "Let's do 20 minutes together."

Visual Timers

Because time blindness is so common, traditional clocks often don't help. Visual timers (like Time Timers or apps with progress circles) give you a *visible* sense of time passing. They're especially helpful for staying on track without constant clock-watching.

Verbal Processing

Talking things out, whether with a friend, a coach, or just yourself, can help bring clarity. Many ADHD brains "think aloud." Use voice notes, talk through your day in the mirror, or explain a problem to a pet if needed. Externalising your thoughts makes them easier to organise.

Dopamine Rewards

ADHD brains are dopamine-hungry. You need novelty, stimulation, and immediate gratification to get going. So give yourself permission to build in rewards; yes, *even for boring things*. Set a timer for 20 minutes of tidying, then watch a YouTube video. Pay a bill, then do something pleasurable. Rewards aren't cheating; they're neuroscience.

Create a Self-Support Menu, Not a Military Routine

One of the biggest mistakes people make when trying to "get organised" is creating a rigid routine they think they *should* follow; only to fall off the wagon within days.

Instead, create a **self-support menu**. Think of it like a toolkit you can dip into, depending on your energy, mood, and capacity that day.

Your menu might include:

- Movement: a 10-minute stretch, a walk, dancing to one song
- Focus boosters: noise-cancelling headphones, a clean workspace, a podcast in the background
- Rest cues: a dark room, herbal tea, permission to nap
- Motivation triggers: setting a timer, texting an accountability buddy, changing your environment

- Emotional regulation: journaling, EFT tapping, a shower, breathing exercises

The idea is not to follow a perfect structure. It's to *have options* that meet you where you are. Different days will have different needs.

You're allowed to try things out, drop what doesn't work, and come back to what does. That *is* success. You don't need to force your brain into a box it was never meant to fit inside.

And most importantly, you deserve systems that *support* your real life, not some idealised version of it. You're **not** failing if a planner didn't change your life. You're **not** failing if a tool worked for a while and then didn't.

7

Chapter 7: ADHD Burnout

Not all burnout is created equal. And if you're living with ADHD, diagnosed or not, there's a specific kind of burnout that hits harder, builds faster, and lasts longer. It doesn't come just from working too much or juggling too many roles. ADHD burnout is what happens when your brain is in a near-constant state of effort. You're navigating executive dysfunction, emotional sensitivity, distraction, and overwhelm every single day. Add masking, shame, and the pressure to "hold it all together," and the weight becomes unbearable.

ADHD burnout is real. It happens after running on fumes for so long that your body, mind, and emotions begin to shut down.

You don't need to be officially diagnosed to feel this kind of exhaustion. You don't need permission to slow down. If you've been living in a state of permanent overdrive, constantly trying to keep up while feeling like you're falling behind, this chapter is for you.

What ADHD Burnout Feels Like

ADHD burnout isn't always loud or obvious. It builds slowly, often over months or years. One day, you're juggling everything; badly, maybe, but still managing. The next, it feels like even brushing your teeth or replying to a simple message is too much. It sneaks in behind the scenes and drains you from the inside out.

Some signs that you might be dealing with ADHD-related burnout:

- You feel mentally foggy, unfocused, or disconnected
- Motivation has completely vanished, even for things you care about
- Small tasks feel insurmountable, and large tasks don't even register
- You crash after bursts of hyper-productivity and struggle to recover
- You're emotionally brittle, crying at little things, snapping at people you love, or feeling numb
- You feel constant guilt for not doing "enough," even when you're barely holding on
- Sleep isn't restorative, and rest doesn't feel restful

This isn't laziness. It's not a lack of ambition or discipline. This is what happens when you've been in a prolonged state of coping, compensating, and pushing past your limits without adequate support or rest.

When You Look Like You're Functioning

One of the hardest parts of ADHD burnout is that it can be invisible. You might still be going to work, replying to messages, picking up the kids, or running a household. From the outside, it looks like you're coping. You probably even hear things like "I don't know how you do it all," while internally, you're barely staying afloat.

This is what we often call *functional burnout.* You're still performing the role, but there's nothing left in the tank. You've been masking the chaos in your brain and the exhaustion in your body for so long that it feels normal. But it isn't. High-functioning doesn't mean thriving. It means surviving while pretending you're fine.

Many women with ADHD hit a breaking point not because they suddenly lost capacity, but because they've been running too long on empty. And no one saw it; maybe not even you.

Why ADHD Brains Are Prone to Burnout

Burnout in ADHD is different because the demands on your brain are different. Managing time, regulating emotions, switching tasks, filtering distractions, and making decisions all require significantly more mental energy when you have ADHD. That's just baseline functioning. Add perfectionism, people pleasing, or masking into the mix, and your nervous system never gets a break.

You're constantly adjusting to the world, adapting your behaviour, trying to stay "on track," and recovering from the emotional fallout when you don't. That effort builds up and takes a toll. Eventually, your brain starts to rebel. You lose motivation, focus, and the ability to cope with even minor stressors. You're not being dramatic. You're burnt out.

It's easy to confuse ADHD burnout with depression, especially when symptoms start to overlap. You might feel flat, foggy, hopeless, or emotionally numb. Burnout often stems from prolonged mental overload and chronic stress without relief.

The key with ADHD burnout is understanding that it isn't simply "doing too much." It's doing too much *without the right kind of support*, for far too long, with a brain that already works overtime just to manage everyday life.

How to Begin Recovering from ADHD Burnout

There's no instant fix. No checklist that will get you back on your feet in three days. But healing begins with a mindset shift: you are not failing, you are fatigued. You are not broken, you are burnt out.

Start small. And when you think you're already doing the bare minimum, go even smaller:

- Take breaks that are actually restful, not scrolling or numbing, but nourishing
- Lower your expectations dramatically and remind yourself

that healing is productive too
- Say no more often, even if it feels uncomfortable
- Let people help you, or at least stop pretending you don't need help
- Find one or two supportive voices, podcasts, online groups; find somewhere where you feel seen
- Track your capacity, not just your tasks. Ask "What can I *realistically* manage today?" and let that be enough

ADHD burnout doesn't go away by pushing harder. It heals with rest, self-awareness, and strategies that work for your actual brain. It requires patience, and that can be hard when your whole identity has been built around pushing through.

But the truth is: the pushing got you here. The healing begins when you stop.

Burnout is not a weakness. It is your body's way of asking you to stop carrying what was never sustainable. If you've been waiting for permission to rest, to slow down, to let go of the pressure, this is it.

You don't have to earn your way to recovery. You just have to begin where you are, and remind yourself, over and over again, that surviving is not the same as thriving. You deserve more than coping.

8

Chapter 8: You Don't Need a Label to Heal

It's human to crave certainty. We want answers, clarity, a neat diagnosis that explains everything and tells us what to do next. Especially when we've spent years feeling like we're the problem, a diagnosis can feel like relief; finally, something *external* to point to.

But the truth is, for many women, that clarity never comes in a clean, "yes or no" package. The lines between ADHD, anxiety, trauma, burnout, hormone disruption, and just plain human struggle are blurry. They overlap. They evolve. And they're shaped as much by your environment and history as by your neurobiology.

That doesn't mean you're stuck. It means you're allowed to start healing *anyway*.

You Don't Need a Diagnosis to Deserve Support

Getting a diagnosis can absolutely be helpful. For some, it brings clarity, validation, and access to treatments or support that would otherwise be hard to reach. It can help you understand your past and make sense of the patterns you've been living with for years. But it's not the only way forward. And more importantly, it's not the only thing that makes your experience real or your needs valid.

If you've been reading this and finding yourself in the stories, symptoms, or struggles described, that is enough. If parts of your life suddenly make more sense through the lens of ADHD or executive dysfunction or chronic burnout, you don't have to wait for someone else to agree with you before you begin supporting yourself. You don't need a letter from a doctor or a report from a specialist to start setting boundaries, building new routines, or treating yourself with more compassion.

Your lived experience matters. You already know what your brain has been asking for. You've probably known for a long time; you were just taught to ignore it, to override it, to push through. But now that you're starting to notice those signals, you get to choose differently.

You are not required to earn support. You do not have to meet a diagnostic threshold to start taking better care of yourself. You are allowed to change how you work, how you rest, how you plan your day, and how you speak to yourself. You are allowed to need things. And you are allowed to give yourself what you need, with or without a formal label.

You are enough. Right now. As you are.

Healing Doesn't Have to Be Perfect

Many of us approach healing the same way we've approached everything else in life: like a project to get right. We want to be the best at it. We make lists. We do the research. We follow the routines, start the journal, set the goals, and build the plan. And when we fall off track, as we inevitably do, we feel like we've failed all over again.

But healing isn't about getting it right. It's not about proving anything. It's not neat, and it's not predictable. Some days you might feel like you're making real progress. Other days, just getting dressed might feel like enough of a win. That's how it works. It's not a sign that you're doing it wrong. It's a sign that you're human.

There's no perfect version of you waiting on the other side of this process. There's just the version of you that feels more supported, more self-aware, and more at peace. And you don't get there by pushing harder. You get there by slowing down. By tuning in. By noticing what you need instead of telling yourself what you "should" be doing.

You don't need to optimise your way out of struggle. You don't need to fix yourself or follow a flawless plan. You just need to meet yourself with patience. Some days, healing looks like setting a boundary. Some days it looks like cancelling plans. Some days, it's a nap. Some days, it's a deep cry. All of that is valid.

You don't have to become someone new to deserve rest and care. You can begin with the self you already are; the one who's been carrying so much for so long. Let her be messy. Let her go gently. Let her have days where nothing gets done but breathing and beginning again.

That's not failure. That's healing.

Finding Your Own Rhythms, Rest Cycles and Boundaries

One of the most liberating things you can do is start listening to *your* body, *your* brain, and *your* needs; rather than trying to force yourself into someone else's version of how life should look. There's so much advice out there telling you how to be productive, how to optimise your mornings, how to structure your days. But what if those systems just don't work for you? What if the problem isn't your discipline, but the shape of the life you've been told you have to live?

Tuning into your own natural rhythms means asking simple but powerful questions:

What feels good?
What feels sustainable?
What drains me?
What supports me?

Maybe your mornings don't need to start with an intense routine, but with quiet. A slow cup of tea. No pressure to hit the ground running. Maybe you focus best in short, focused bursts rather than long, uninterrupted sessions. Maybe you need built-in buffers between tasks so your brain has space to reset. Maybe it's not just time you need to protect with boundaries, but energy.

None of that makes you unreliable. It doesn't mean you're lazy or not trying hard enough. It means you're paying attention to how you actually work, instead of shaming yourself for not being able to work like everyone else.

The more you listen to what your mind and body are asking for, the more stable things begin to feel. You don't crash as often. You don't spiral into overwhelm as easily. You begin to trust yourself. And that's when things start to shift; not because you've changed who you are, but because you've finally stopped fighting it.

Radical Self-Compassion

If there's one thing that truly transforms how you live with ADHD, burnout, or emotional overwhelm, it's this: **radical self-compassion**.

And by radical, I mean brave. I mean choosing to treat yourself with care even when everything inside you says you don't deserve it. I mean refusing to measure your worth by your output, even when the world around you still does.

Radical self- compassion says:

- I forgive myself for the times I didn't know better or didn't have the tools
- I give myself permission to need support, without guilt
- I will not punish myself for how I'm wired or how long things take me
- I choose to meet myself with patience and softness, even when it feels unfamiliar

You've spent so much time fighting with your own brain. Pushing through, masking, shaming yourself into trying harder. But what if the thing you needed most was not more discipline, but more understanding?

What if you stopped trying to force change through self-criticism, and started creating change through self-respect?

The moment you stop being your own harshest critic and start becoming your own ally, everything begins to feel different.

This is your permission slip: to stop striving, to start listening, and to trust that you are allowed to support yourself; here, now, as you are.

9

Afterword

You're Not Alone, and You're Not Broken

If you've made it this far, take a moment to breathe. You've just walked through some of the most tangled, painful, and deeply personal terrain a woman can face; the inner landscape of feeling like you're failing, when all along, you've been carrying more than anyone realised.

You are *not* broken. You are not lazy. You are not imagining it. And most importantly, **you are not alone**.

Whether or not you walk away from this book with a clear diagnosis, you've already taken the first step that matters most: **validation**. You've questioned the story you've been told about yourself. You've peeled back the layers of shame and started to ask, "What if I'm not the problem?"

That is powerful.

Reflection Prompts for Moving Forward

What behaviours or feelings in this book did I most relate to; and what might they be trying to tell me?

When in my life have I felt most aligned, focused, or myself? What conditions made that possible?

What tools, rhythms, or boundaries could I experiment with this week to make life a little softer?

Where am I holding onto guilt or shame about how I function; and what would it feel like to let some of that go?

What does support *look like for me right now, and how can I ask for it without apology?*

You're Not Meant to Do This Alone

Whether you're just beginning to untangle things or you're halfway through a transformation, you're not the only one walking this path. Thousands of women are waking up to the same realisations. They're asking the same questions and sharing the same stories.

Here are some resources to explore, if and when you're ready:

Books

- *ADHD 2.0* – Dr. Edward Hallowell & Dr. John Ratey
- *Women with ADHD* – Sari Solden
- *Burnout: The Secret to Unlocking the Stress Cycle* – Emily & Amelia Nagoski
- *Driven to Distraction* – Edward Hallowell
- *The Body Keeps the Score* – Bessel van der Kolk (for trauma; informed context)

Podcasts

- **ADHD for Smart Ass Women** – Tracy Otsuka
- **The ADHD Women's Wellbeing Podcast** – Kate Moryoussef
- **Hacking Your ADHD** – William Curb
- **Seize the Yay** – Sarah Holloway (for burnout and balance)

Screeners & Tools

- WHO Adult ADHD Self; Report Scale (ASRS)
- ADHD 2.0 Quick Screener
- Time Timer app (for visual time management)
- Notion, Todoist, or Trello (for ADHD; friendly planning)

Communities & Support

- **ADHD Babes (UK)** – A support group for Black women & non; binary people with ADHD
- **The Neurodivergent Women's Circle** – Various local and online meetups
- **Reddit**: r/ADHDwomen
- **Instagram Accounts**: @adhd_love, @the_mini_adhd_coach, @katiemaycock

www.ingramcontent.com/pod-product-compliance
Lightning Source LLC
LaVergne TN
LVHW022314200926
848481LV00004B/1344